Patrick Mahomes: The Inspiring Story of One of Football's Superstar Quarterbacks

An Unauthorized Biography

By: Clayton Geoffreys

Table of Contents

Foreword

Few African-American quarterbacks have won the Most Valuable Player award before -- Patrick Mahomes is one of those few individuals. In just his first few seasons playing professional football, Mahomes has won a Super Bowl, a Super Bowl MVP award, as well as a Most Valuable Player award. It should come as no surprise that Mahomes was rewarded for his efforts in 2020, as he signed a 10-year contract extension with the potential of earning over $500 million. Mahomes has a bright future ahead of him, and it'll be exciting to see how many more Super Bowl titles and MVPs he can chase over the course of his career. Thank you for purchasing *Patrick Mahomes: The Inspiring Story of One of Football's Superstar Quarterbacks*. In this unauthorized biography, we will learn Patrick Mahomes' incredible life story and impact on the game of football. Hope you enjoy and if you do, please do not forget to leave a review!

Also, check out my website at claytongeoffreys.com to join my exclusive list where I let you know about my latest books. To thank you for your purchase, you can go to my site to download a free copy of *33 Life Lessons: Success Principles, Career Advice & Habits of Successful People.* In the book, you'll learn from some of the greatest thought leaders of different industries on what it takes to become successful and how to live a great life. I'll also send you a few more sports biographies for you to enjoy.

Cheers,

Clayton Geoffreys

Visit me at www.claytongeoffreys.com

Introduction

In the 2017 NFL Draft, Patrick Mahomes II sat at his table waiting for his name to be called. With the second pick, the Chicago Bears passed on him and took quarterback Mitchell Trubisky out of North Carolina. The Jacksonville Jaguars felt they already had their future with Blake Bortles and took running back Leonard Fournette instead. The Jets were okay with Geno Smith and Josh McCown and instead took safety Jamal Adams. The Bengals decided to hold onto Andy Dalton and drafted wide receiver John Ross.[i]

It was like heaven for the Kansas City Chiefs. They had traded with the Buffalo Bills for the 10th overall pick and when their turn came up, Mahomes was still there. So was Deshaun Watson of Clemson, but they felt Mahomes was a no-brainer. They believed Mahomes was a potential Pro Bowler who could win them a Super Bowl in two or three years.

And they were spot on.

Three years later, Mahomes had made many of those nine teams that passed on him regret it. How do you think the Bears felt? Trubisky is not even their starting quarterback anymore. Or the Jaguars, who have floundered with the quarterback position since 2015. Blake Bortles, their guy in 2017, is now on the Rams. The Jets may have been the team that felt the sickest. Their quarterback play was so bad in 2017 that they drafted Sam Darnold in 2018. They could have picked a top quarterback in 2017 but instead passed on one. The player they did draft in 2017, Jamal Adams, is now on the Seahawks!

Then there were the Chiefs, who drafted Mahomes and got to see him win the 2018 NFL Most Valuable Player Award and hold up the Lombardi Trophy in 2020.

It did not take long for the Chiefs general manager to be completely on board with Mahomes. After the 2017 NFL Combine in Indianapolis, he saw all that he needed to. "He's one of the best players I ever saw," Brett Veach said.[ii]

At the time, everyone thought that was merely "general manager speak." But over the years, people realized he was 100% right.

"The fact he was there with the 10th pick was like winning the lottery," Veach said. "I couldn't believe it."

Even after winning the Super Bowl in February 2020, head coach Andy Reid said Mahomes still had a long way to go until he reached his potential. That is scary to fathom. Arguably the best quarterback in the NFL still had a lot of growth left in him?

Mahomes grew up with athletic skills thanks to his father. Patrick Mahomes, Sr. was a professional baseball player from 1992 until 2003, playing mostly with the Twins but also spending time with Boston, the New York Mets, Pittsburgh, Texas, and the Chicago Cubs. While his numbers were not outstanding, he did make a name for himself during his tenure with the Mets, going 8-0 in 1999 and playing in the World Series in 2000 against the Yankees.[iii]

Patrick spent most of his life living in Texas and playing multiple sports growing up, particularly baseball. It was not until high school that he started playing football. Just like his father, he was a natural athlete. He had one of the strongest arms in all of Texas. Coming out of high school, he was drafted by the Detroit Tigers and had the opportunity to skip college and go right to the minor leagues. He was offered a contract but held off on signing. It just so happened that Patrick loved football even more, and felt he had a better chance to succeed in it than baseball. After an incredible high school career, he was recruited by a few schools but chose to stay close to home and play quarterback at Texas Tech University. Just like he did in high school, he set records, some of which still stand and may never be broken.

Mahomes had still considered baseball as a potential option in the back of his mind while he played at Texas Tech, but the more he played football in college and achieved success, the less interested he was in going the baseball route. In 2016, he announced he was quitting baseball to focus strictly on football.

Mahomes shined with the Red Raiders. He was given the nickname "Showtime" after he continuously put on shows for the crowd with his incredible performances. He set the all-time single-game record for 819 yards passing in a game. He had other games where he threw for over 600 and 700 yards. He won the Sammy Baugh Trophy in 2016 for being the best passer in college football. While some thought it was just the superior makeup of the offense going up against weak Big 12 defenses that made Mahomes stand out, some NFL scouts felt it was much more.[iv]

Mahomes decided after his junior year to go pro and entered the NFL Draft where he was selected by the

Chiefs with that 10th overall pick. While he impressed in the preseason, he rode the bench as the backup to Alex Smith during the first year, not starting until the final game of his rookie season. But the Chiefs were excited enough by what they saw that they made Mahomes the team's starter in 2018. That year, he won the NFL MVP and took his team all the way to the AFC Championship. The following year, he suffered an injury that kept him out for much of the first half of the season, but he healed up just in time to take the helm for the team's playoff run. The Chiefs beat the San Francisco 49ers in Super Bowl LIV to win their second-ever World Championship. Mahomes was named the Super Bowl MVP.[iii]

Only two years in as a full-time starter, Mahomes already held a number of records. He threw the most touchdown passes (10) in his first three career games. He threw the most touchdown passes through the first eight career games. He was the first player to throw over 3,000 yards in his first 10 NFL games. His 31 touchdown passes in his first 10 games was also a record.[iv]

Already three years into the NFL, Mahomes has accomplished more than most other quarterbacks in the league and is likely on his way to a Hall-of-Fame career.

Mahomes' success goes beyond what you see on the field. He has been a role model for young athletes everywhere who want to be great in sports. In an age where most young athletes are being inundated by the influences of alcohol, drugs, division, and hateful rhetoric, Mahomes has stayed well above all that. He has taught kids how to focus on the positives, not the negatives. He has inspired kids to work hard and ignore the distractions around them. He has motivated kids to have the attitude of a winner and put your team above your own accomplishments. Over time, Patrick's coaches and teammates have developed the highest level of respect for him because of the exemplary way he handles himself on and off the field as well as the fact that he has shown himself to be an exceptional leader.

"He's a great kid, first of all," Mahomes' head coach Andy Reid said. "He understands the leadership role he's been put in by position and how important that is, and he's got that innate ability to lead. So, you give him a little guideline on that, and he takes it and goes."[v]

The best part about it all is that Mahomes' story is still ongoing. The future Hall-of-Fame quarterback is still learning. The leader is still maturing. The sport of football is still getting better because of the 2019 Super Bowl MVP. The future is ripe with achievements to come and we are excited to watch this remarkable young man's career unfold.

Chapter 1: Early Childhood

Patrick Lavon Mahomes II was born on September 17, 1995, in Tyler, Texas to Pat Mahomes and Randi Martin. He was born of mixed race to an African American father and white mother, much like baseball icon Derek Jeter. While his nickname may now be "Showtime" for his football stardom, growing up he was known as "Pattycakes."[v]

The oldest of three children, Patrick grew up playing baseball just like his dad. He showed tremendous athleticism at a very early age and was mentored by his father to one day become a professional baseball player. He did not play organized football at all as a child, not even Pop Warner.[v]

It was baseball which was Patrick's obsession growing up, with basketball a close second. A lot of it was fueled by his father, who always brought his son to the games. Many times during pre-game warmups and batting practice, Pat would bring little Patrick out onto the field and have him shag balls hit by the other guys and play around with the other players on the team.

"He loved baseball," Pat said. "I bought him a plastic bat with one of those little balls and he would never go to bed. He always wanted to hit with it, even late into the night."[vi]

Growing up, Patrick developed a passion for competition. He did not just love to play baseball; he was hardcore competitive in basketball, golf, the high jump, and even table tennis.

Patrick was not influenced in baseball just by his father, either. He also idolized greats like Derek Jeter and Alex Rodriguez growing up and they motivated him to become a baseball player when he was older.

"I saw those two (Jeter and Rodriguez) at the top of their game and how much work they put in," Mahomes said. "I think that instilled in me at a young age that it's not about being at the top. It's about the process of getting there."[vii]

Many times, the best athletes in the world have their own idols they look up to. Many of the best current NBA stars looked up to Michael Jordan as a child. Many golfers coming up idolized Tiger Woods or Jack Nicklaus. Many football players wanted to be Tom Brady. Pat Mahomes, Sr. wanted to be Kirby Puckett. Young kids now want to be like Patrick Mahomes.

Along with his father, Mahomes spent a lot of time as a kid around Alex Rodriguez. According to Pat, "A-Rod" was a huge influence on him and inspired a passion for sports and the desire to work hard to be the best. Patrick's godfather, LaTroy Hawkins, also taught him how to be professional and what to do and not to do.[viii]

The more Patrick was involved in sports at a young age, the more he learned about the work ethic involved. His parents instilled in him the importance of going above and beyond in everything, including schoolwork. Patrick was a straight-A student in school, and as he became involved in Little League baseball, he was the best player on his team, always wanting to stay after practice to keep trying to improve.

"The first time on that baseball field, you could tell he was the best player out there even though he was the youngest player out there," Pat said. "This is a boy who was shagging fly balls off big-league bats and making catches when he was just five years old."[viii]

Fans first got to see young Patrick on the baseball field just before Game 3 of the 2000 World Series between the Yankees and the Mets at Shea Stadium. At that time, Pat pitched for the Mets, and as was the custom, young Patrick was out with the players shagging fly balls.

"He was running in the outfield tracking down deep hits and making catches that major leaguers won't make and he was just five years old," Mets pitcher Mike Hampton said, who used to shag balls in the outfield with him. "He was trying to jump over me and other players to make the catch. It was unreal. He was also throwing rockets back into the infield. You could tell right then this kid was special. The athleticism...I mean, he had it all."[ix]

It is similar to the story of Ken Griffey, Jr. who also learned how to be a great baseball player by shagging fly balls and being around professional athletes as a young boy while his father played with Pete Rose, Johnny Bench, and the Cincinnati Big Red Machine. Many of the great athletes who had fathers who made it to the top were exposed to being around the best and they got a chance to work with elite athletes that other kids don't. It gave them a distinct advantage.

"These kids—the Ken Griffeys and the guys that just hung around clubhouses and stuff like that, you just kind of get comfortable in the situation where you're not overwhelmed," Hampton said. "I think all of those things led to where he's at now, not only in his physical skills but his mentality."[ix]

The New York Post printed a picture during the 2000 World Series that showed young Patrick running with Hampton trying to track down a deep 300-foot shot in batting practice.[ix]

As Patrick grew older, his arm got stronger. As he played organized baseball as a child, he played all positions. When he pitched, his fastball was clocked at over 78 miles-per-hour before he even got to high school. He also played shortstop and would rifle balls to first base.[vi]

At six years old, Patrick had to go through a rough patch in his family. His parents, Pat and Randi, divorced and went their separate ways. Fortunately, unlike some parents that divorce, both Pat and Randi were respectful of Patrick and their children and remained friends after their divorce. Both helped support their kids through elementary, middle, and high school.

Patrick's brother, Jackson, was also very athletic growing up but was not as into baseball as his brother and father. Instead, Jackson was obsessed with basketball growing up and spent his younger days on the hardcourt.[iv]

As for football, Patrick always had a curiosity to try it out, but his father wanted to keep him focused on baseball.

"Baseball had been pretty much his whole life growing up, and he always played basketball, too," Pat said. "Those were his two sports. I was trying to keep him from playing football."[x]

Amazingly, the future-best quarterback in the NFL hardly touched a pigskin until he became a teenager. Instead, he was focused strictly on baseball and had high hopes of becoming a star pitcher or infielder in high school. But as he got closer to high school, his friends started to talk to him about playing football. Still, while there was some temptation, there was also the focus on baseball and his father perpetually in his ear trying to groom him as a future baseball star.

While he was not religious in his earliest years, Patrick developed a love for the Christian faith in middle school and began going to church on a regular basis. He attributes a lot of his early success to his faith in God and prayer. He was also into going out and playing with his friends in his free time and playing a variety of other less mainstream sports like ping pong and racquetball. His parents always pushed him to focus on his schoolwork first, however, and sports second; social time came third.[v]

As Patrick finished junior high school, he was about to enter a new phase of his life—high school. It was there where everything would change forever.

Chapter 2: High School Career

Patrick Mahomes enrolled in Whitehouse High School in Whitehouse, Texas. Going in, he was seen as a star athlete, not only because of who his father was but also because of the skills that others saw him exemplify in baseball.

But Patrick wanted to play everything in high school. If there were 12 seasons made up of different sports, Patrick would play 12 sports. When asked what his favorite sport was, his response was always the same: "Whatever is in season."[x]

During that first year, he decided to give football a try for the first time. It was not what his father wanted, but at the same time, his parents encouraged him to explore what *he* wanted. With his friends talking him into trying out, he decided to step onto the field for the first time in his life. That first season, he played as a defensive back for the team. When winter came around, he played basketball and started as the team's point guard as a freshman. In the spring, it was baseball season where he played shortstop and made the varsity team.

Mahomes was the school's star freshman athlete that first year. Other kids and coaches saw big things coming for him. He radiated potential and was particularly impressive on the basketball court and the baseball field with his tremendous arm.

"I remember he used to throw these diagonal no-look passes on the court where he knew someone was going to end up that just amazed everyone," Mahomes' basketball coach Ryan Tomlin said. "These were things you couldn't teach. He just had natural instincts. You see him on the football field today and you saw the same things on the basketball court in high school."[xi]

As a shortstop, he used to throw balls to first base with such force that it hurt the first baseman's hand. There were times where coaches had to bring ice out to heal the hand of whoever was playing that position and catching balls from Patrick.[xi]

Those first couple seasons, as good as Mahomes was in baseball, Tomlin said Mahomes also had the talent to be a star NBA player. He had the vision of a Magic Johnson, just knowing where players were going to be. He also had incredible spatial awareness and had an unorthodox jump shot. Mahomes had the uncanny ability to score when the team needed him the most.

Then Mahomes' sophomore season came around. Adam Cook, the Whitehouse football coach, had seen what Mahomes was doing on the basketball court and baseball diamond with his arm. He saw this kid had rare athleticism. When people talked about Mahomes at that point, it was his baseball and basketball skills that were impressing people. Cook thought he could change that. He saw something in Mahomes that was special and decided to change his position from defensive back to quarterback where he could use that very apparent strength in his arm to full advantage.

Cook spent Mahomes' sophomore season teaching him some basic principles but never overwhelmed him with mechanical instruction. He felt that would come with time, given his athletic talents. Basics needed to come first. While Patrick's father was not fully on-board with Patrick playing quarterback, at the time, he let it play out.[xi]

Mahomes began to feel comfortable at the position as the summer progressed. However, Cook urged Mahomes to continue to play basketball and baseball even after he became the team's starting quarterback, saying that the other sports would only help him become a better quarterback in his junior season. Mahomes' godfather, LaTroy Hawkins, tried to convince Mahomes to focus squarely on basketball, saying he felt it was his best sport of all three.[xii] But Mahomes was more focused on becoming a better quarterback at the time, something he was just starting to learn and enjoy.

As Mahomes developed into a quarterback, he had an unorthodox style about him, likely because he did not grow up playing the sport and played quarterback much like he did basketball. He was a runner and threw the ball many times on the run and in unique situations. While that unusual style would indeed become successful for him in high school, many thought he would never make it past high school as a quarterback because of it.

Bobby Stroupe was Mahomes' coach since he was in fourth grade, helping with all sports he played. In football, he worked with Mahomes and agreed with Cook to focus on the basic principles rather than loading him with technique.

"Instead of trying to get him to do the things that people think make quarterbacks unique and special, we just continued to bore into him the things that made

Patrick unique and special," Stroupe said. "If you really watch him play, he's an incredibly creative person. Someone like that has to be trained in a way that supports his athleticism. His athleticism does not fit in a bucket. He's not a big overhand, throw-down guy. His feet don't set like normal quarterbacks."[xi]

Sometimes the best players are the best because they do it *their* way and not necessarily the "right" way. For example, Ichiro became a star hitter despite doing absolutely the opposite of how coaches typically teach you to hit growing up. He had a golf-inspired pendulum swing with the bat that worked for him and made him successful. And speaking of golf, have you ever watched Jim Furyk swing a golf club? It is the most unorthodox swing in the world, but yet he has won a U.S. Open and has been one of the best pro golfers in the world. And then there is tennis star Rafael Nadal, who was also different in that he did not have a dominating serve like most all other great tennis players, but he proved you can win and become one of the greatest players ever with speed on the court and a powerful forehand, not a serve.

This was Mahomes. He was different at quarterback. He was not about having the perfect technique. He did not need to be trained to throw it like Tom Brady or Peyton Manning. He did not want to be the next Joe Montana or Brett Favre. He wanted to be the first Patrick Mahomes. He did not want to adjust something he felt comfortable with and was working for him.

Many felt that Mahomes avoiding textbook mechanics was crucial to his development. Focusing too much on them could have ruined him as a quarterback and hurt him in his other sports as well. It could have destroyed the way he threw the ball to first base and it could have caused him to lose his skills as a passer on the basketball court.

"Even when the textbook is reasonable, it does not nearly encompass the variation of things that work," David Epstein said, a sports scientist who has studied many athletes and their development. "It's sort of like showing an average of some population and not including the incredible variance, which is often where the truth really lies."[xi]

One of the best things that Mahomes learned while playing all three sports early in high school was competitiveness and leadership. Whenever he was taken out in a basketball game, he went right to the coaches and sat next to them, asking how he could improve his play the next time. He always stayed after baseball practice to work on whatever weakness he felt in his hitting or fielding. With football, he was working overtime to prove that his style can work and to become a better thrower. Many say that Mahomes would not have been the quarterback he is today without playing all those sports. They seemed to only make him a better athlete moving forward and taught him the other aspects of the game that make players great, like leading by example and showing good sportsmanship and teamwork.

Mahomes had the arm. Some said it was the strongest in all of Texas. At 6'3", he had the size. He had the athleticism. He had the pedigree. It was only a matter of time—in between his sophomore and junior year everything would start to come together and he would dominate at the quarterback position.

However, Mahomes was not sure at the time if football was for him. While he enjoyed the new position at quarterback, he was not yet certain that he was comfortable in it. He felt like baseball was more for him. It was what he grew up playing. It was what his dad wanted. By his junior year, he wanted to have a better vision of his future and the sport he would play as an adult. He was leaning towards giving up football.

"Before his junior year in high school, he came to me that summer wanting to quit football," Randi Martin said. "I told him you're going to regret it if you quit."[xviii]

While Pat, Sr. wanted baseball for Patrick, Randi felt Mahomes had a future in football and that he could excel at it.

In 2012, his junior season, high school camp broke and Mahomes was implemented as the team's No. 1 quarterback with no competition. Most of the people who knew Patrick figured that once he got the starting job, he was going to become a talked-about player throughout all of Texas. This was a kid that did not know how to fail. He had the most incredible athletic genes of anyone. In fact, had he focused solely on golf in high school, his friends and family felt he could have topped Tiger Woods' records.

That junior season, Mahomes lit it up. He broke all sorts of school records, throwing for 3,839 yards and tossing 46 touchdowns. You might think that any player with those numbers would have college coaches all over the country flocking to games and begging him to accept their scholarship. However, Mahomes was not getting many offers. He was getting most looked at by Texas Christian University (TCU) and Texas Tech. The next month, Oklahoma State also talked to him and offered him a scholarship. But outside of that, most were looking at him for his baseball and basketball skills, not his football prowess. What was even odder was that Whitehouse had great quarterbacks in the past that had sent talent to schools like Oklahoma and Texas A&M. In the end, Mahomes got just three scholarship offers from universities for football.

One who wanted Mahomes badly was Kliff Kingsbury, the head coach of the Texas Tech Red Raiders. Kingsbury was an offensive guy who once played quarterback himself at Texas Tech. The school is known for grooming gunslingers and piling up points against Big 12 opponents, but Kingsbury wanted someone who could also run and make plays with his legs. The minute he saw Mahomes, he was enamored with him. After his junior season, Texas Tech made an offer to Mahomes.

"I just remember seeing Patrick with his eyes wide-open and excited about how much they threw the ball at Tech because we did the exact same thing in high school," Coleman Patterson said, Mahomes' childhood friend and high school teammate. "He also hit it off with Coach Kingsbury. He was enticed by the offer. Texas Tech was kind of a no-brainer for him. But baseball was still in the back of his mind."[xi]

Baseball was still what Patrick's dad wanted for him. He had groomed Patrick as a child to be a Major League player. It was his dream and he was afraid that if he focused on football after high school, he would not reach his full potential like he would with baseball.

Spencer Shaw was a friend and classmate of Patrick Mahomes. When his senior year began, he was approached by the yearbook staff to answer the question, "What do you look forward to most at your high school reunion?"

"Seeing Patrick Mahomes' Super Bowl ring," Shaw said, which was printed in the 2014 yearbook.[xiv]

Patrick's Decision

As Mahomes entered his final year of high school, a year that is typically one of the best of any teenager's life, an unusual drama surrounded Whitehouse High School that year... Which sport would Patrick Mahomes choose?

After his junior season in football, he had already committed to play football for Texas Tech but that did not mean the door was shut on his other two sports. He was an All-Star point guard on the basketball team and could have landed a scholarship there if he wanted it. Then there was baseball where MLB teams and college scouts were coming to all of his games to watch him play. He was regarded as one of the top hitters and pitchers in all of Texas.

His senior year in football, Mahomes started in all 13 games for Whitehouse. He shattered the records that he set during his junior season. He threw for an incredible 4,619 yards (more than 355 yds/game), and broke his own touchdown record by 4, passing for 50 of them. But what was most impressive was how he used his legs. In 2012, Mahomes ran for just 258 yards in the 12 games he started. After committing to Texas Tech and talking with Kingsbury, he wanted to use his mobility more. In 2013, he ran for 940 yards. He had transitioned from a drop back passer to a dangerous mobile quarterback with a lethal arm.[xix]

Kingsbury was impressed as he watched Mahomes progress to more of a dual-threat quarterback and was excited to see him excel moving forward. He knew big things were on the way. But he was still worried Mahomes would ultimately choose baseball over football given his family past.

Mahomes did not play basketball his senior season, wanting to focus more on just football and baseball. During baseball season, he helped lead his team to a 23-8 record and was the team's star pitcher. He threw a no-hitter one game where he had 16 strikeouts and nearly hit for the cycle. His fastball got up to 93 mph that senior season and he was hitting .450. He was among the top three dozen prospects and was all but guaranteed to be picked in the Major League Baseball Draft coming up that summer.[xv]

However, when the draft came, teams passed on Mahomes, thinking he was not going to play baseball. Word has already spread among all the Major League teams that Mahomes desired to play college football over at Texas Tech rather than baseball, but would go back to baseball should his football career fail. In fact, when Baseball America printed their scouting report on Mahomes, it stated that very fact:

"Mahomes' father of the same name spent parts of 11 seasons in the major leagues and was still pitching in independent ball until 2009. His son has a bigger, more physical frame at a listed 6'2", 214 pounds and has shown a low-90s fastball on the mound while also showcasing excellent arm strength when he plays right field. Some evaluators like him better as a hitter who is an average runner with plus raw power from a raw offensive approach. Mahomes appears to prefer football, however, with good reason. He's a quarterback committed to Texas Tech." – Baseball America[xviii]

That kind of non-commitment crushed his draft stock. Mahomes dropped all the way to the 37th round where the Detroit Tigers selected him.[xv]

Mahomes was enticed by the Tigers offer, but despite his father's wishes for him to play baseball, Mahomes told the Tigers that he wanted to play college football at Texas Tech. He told the Tigers at the time that he would still consider playing baseball as well but wanted to focus on college first and foremost.

"I would be lying if I said that I wasn't disappointed at first," Pat, Sr. said. "But I believed in him. I knew deep down that if he were to commit to football and want to be a star quarterback, he would be one. He had so much athleticism and drive in him, whatever he wanted to do, he could do. I told him I would always support him no matter what. If that's what he wanted, I'd behind him 100%."[xi]

It is what a son wants. Not having his father by his side would have crushed Patrick and made football harder for him. It would have left doubt in his mind. He knew his mother already wanted him to play football, but he knew his dad wanted him to follow in his footsteps. Having his dad come around and support him was vital for Patrick.

Tim Grieve, the Tigers scout who had recommended drafting Mahomes, had watched the young star throughout most of his high school career play baseball and impress the fans in not just baseball, but in football and basketball as well.

"He was the best player on the field or on the court in three different sports," Grieve said. "It wasn't like you were just talking about one sport, one position. I'm pretty sure he would've been good at whatever he wanted to do. And you see the smile."[xv]

Grieve thought Mahomes had the arm to throw in the mid-to-high 90s. However, he knew that the chance of him choosing baseball over football was a longshot. After all, Mahomes was already on campus at Texas Tech when Grieve called him to tell him that they had drafted him.

"You knew what it was," Grieve said. "This was a kid who wanted to play football. The draft pick at the time was more [about], 'You deserve this.' Let's be that team that starts laying the foundation so if he goes to Texas Tech and football does not work, or if he decides he likes baseball, you've already started the relationship."[xv]

It was basically an insurance policy. Grieve said that Mahomes was the kind of guy who you just enjoyed watching. It was not just about his talent. He said the kid just loved playing. He always carried around a smile wherever he went and had fun. It is that kind of player any team would dream of having in their lineup.[xv] Oh yeah, and the fact that he was one of the top prospects and had one of the best arms in the country may have had something to do with it also.

Mahomes was not the first multi-sport college player that Grieve tried to persuade to play baseball. He also recruited Matthew Stafford, who was a star baseball and football player, along with Carl Crawford, who also had scholarships to play both college football and basketball. While Grieve was unsuccessful with

Stafford, who ended up signing with Georgia and then the Detroit Lions, he was successful persuading Crawford, who became a second-round pick and future All-Star with the Tampa Bay Rays. He also recruited Clayton Kershaw who now plays for the Dodgers.[xv]

Tim Tadlock, the manager for the Texas Tech Red Raiders baseball team, also had high hopes of Mahomes playing baseball. Knowing he had already signed a scholarship to play football, he hoped he could persuade Mahomes to play two sports in college.

"I saw him as a ninth-grader," Tadlock said. "If you ever saw him play, you'd never forget it."[xvi]

Mahomes met with Tadlock and the Texas Tech coaching staff and decided to play college baseball with the Red Raiders after football season was over.

But as the summer of 2014 arrived, Mahomes had put baseball in the back of his mind. His focus was on one thing: college football.

Chapter 3: College Football Career

Patrick Mahomes may have been a star at Whitehouse High School, but entering college, there were very few expectations of him. He was listed as a three-star recruit and ranked as the 398th-ranked incoming freshman, according to 247Sports' Composite Rankings. The fact that only three schools offered him a scholarship spoke volumes about what college scouts thought of him.[xviii]

Why were the rankings so low? For starters, his technique was different. He played to his own style, not the style that quarterbacks are taught. There was also the feeling that he lacked commitment because of baseball and that he was not going to go all-in as a football player. He had never announced that he would quit baseball forever. He just put it on hold until the spring. Additionally, Mahomes just started playing quarterback two years ago. All the other guys that scouts pursued more enthusiastically had been playing it most of their lives.

"I think they missed because he never had the coaching all those other guys had," LaTroy Hawkins said. "He never went to those quarterback camps; he never did that."[xviii]

Mahomes began the 2014 college football season on the bench as a freshman, backing up starter Davis Webb. While Mahomes at times outshined Webb in preseason practices and scrimmages, Kingsbury thought it was still too early to throw Mahomes in the lineup. He wanted to coach him up and give him a chance to develop behind Webb before he faced the fire. The Red Raiders also had Vincent Testaverde, son of former college football and NFL quarterback Vinny Testaverde.

Then there was high school superstar Jarrett Stidham, who is the current quarterback for the New England Patriots at the time of this writing. The Red Raiders had signed the 5-star recruit in March 2014 and had their eyes set on him being the future star at Texas Tech despite their hopes for Mahomes.

Kingsbury's goal was to have the best quarterbacks possible and then play the best, and recruiting a 5-star talent like Stidham to play alongside Mahomes was what he wanted. More than anything, though, Kingsbury was also concerned that Mahomes would not commit to football and wanted insurance. He knew Mahomes was looking at playing baseball for the Red Raiders in the spring. He also did not know how his out-of-the-box playing style would translate to the college game at the time.

The Red Raiders struggled that 2014 season under Webb as the starting quarterback. They were 3-5 in eight games and had racked up an embarrassing loss, 82-37, to TCU. The offense was scoring 30 points per game, but defensively, they were giving up close to 50 points per game. Mahomes saw his first action against

Oklahoma State, going 2-for-5 for 20 yards and a touchdown. He also saw some action against Kansas State and in the loss to TCU when Webb got hurt.[xix]

In the ninth game of the season against the Texas Longhorns, Kingsbury decided to give Mahomes his first shot at starting a game. Mahomes would split some time with Testaverde. Mahomes had a solid debut, going 13-for-21 and throwing for 109 yards in the team's 34-13 loss to the Longhorns. But Kingsbury liked what he saw.[xix]

"There was a spark in that game," Kingsbury later said. "No, he wasn't able to pile up a lot of points or lead us back to win, but there was that spark, that energy when he was in the game. It was a different feeling. The guys on the field trusted him because of his leadership out there. You knew that with more playing time, better things would come."[xvi]

After the Texas game, Kingsbury decided to keep Mahomes as a starter and he never turned back. In a home game against Big 12 power Oklahoma, it was expected that the Red Raiders would have their struggles, but instead, they got something different. Mahomes shined, making plays with his arms and his legs. Mahomes was 27-for-50 throwing for 393 yards and tossing 4 touchdowns while finishing with a quarterback rating of 146.4. Despite the 42-30 loss to the Sooners, the Mahomes era in Lubbock had taken off.[xix]

In his next start on the road against Iowa State, Mahomes continued to develop and flourish. He went 23-for-35 and tossed another 4 touchdowns, finishing with a quarterback rating of 176.4. Better yet, he helped lead the Red Raiders down the field to win the game in the fourth quarter, 34-31.[xix]

In his final game of the season against Baylor, Mahomes was expected to struggle against the fifth-ranked Bears, who were the Big 12's best team that season. Defensively, the Red Raiders could not handle the powerful Bears offensive attack, but the story of the game was Mahomes. Fans were mesmerized as they watched the freshman quarterback make throws on the run, deep throws over the top, and scramble for first downs. He threw sidearm, overhand, and even added an underhanded toss. He was slinging it all over the place. It was reminiscent of Brett Favre in his prime.

The Bears' defense could not stop him. Mahomes was making plays left and right and in the end, threw for 598 yards and tossed 6 touchdowns. Despite losing 48-46 in a thriller to the No. 5 Bears, it was truly Mahomes' "coming out party." Stidham was on the sidelines watching his future school and Mahomes have one of the best college games ever for a quarterback. Shortly after, Stidham de-committed from Texas Tech and later signed on to play football at Auburn. Some might say he was stunned at what he saw and thought he could not compete with that talent.[xvii]

Mahomes ended the season on top and gave the Red Raiders high hopes for the 2015 season. However, Mahomes delivered on his promise to give baseball a try at Texas Tech as well. On Feb. 21, 2015, Mahomes started for the Red Raiders against Northern Illinois. It was his first start after high school—and his last.

Mahomes' took the mound and struggled. It was his worst ever game as a pitcher. He threw just 15 pitches and faced 3 batters. He walked two of them and pegged the other. He came out of the game and was supported by the rest of the team but did not want to pitch again.[xviii]

Mahomes sat on the bench for two other games, getting in as a pinch-hitter and seeing two at-bats, both of which he recorded outs in. After the third game, Mahomes realized baseball was not for him anymore. He left the Red Raiders baseball team to focus squarely on football. His college baseball career thus ended with him leaving with a 99.00 ERA.[xviii]

Soon thereafter, Mahomes called the Detroit Tigers up and told them his baseball career was over and he was negating on his contract. He would be concentrating full-time on football. His new dream was to play in the NFL.

With just one sport now on Mahomes' mind, he was purely focused on football and it showed on the field. He was progressing at incredible levels. His sophomore season featured some incredible highlights and games that may never go unmatched.

In his first two games that season, Mahomes threw eight touchdowns and helped his team get off to a 2-0 start. However, they would go into Arkansas as a heavy underdog. A year ago, they were embarrassed by the Razorbacks on their home field, 49-21. But with Mahomes now leading the way, times were different.

It would go down as one of Mahomes' best games, not so much from a statistical standpoint, but from an efficiency one. He only threw for 243 yards against the

SEC defense, his second-lowest total of the season, but he threw just four incompletions. He was 26-for-30, and despite feeling pressure, used his legs just like his coach wanted. He ran 10 times for 58 yards, two of those rushes for touchdowns.[xvii]

In the end, the Red Raiders shocked the Razorbacks on their home field, 35-24, led by Mahomes, who was developing as a leader on the team. They were now 3-0.[xvii]

The Red Raiders went through a bit of a rough stretch after that, losing five of their next seven games, but Mahomes continued to put up great numbers. He threw for 415 yards and 3 touchdowns in the team's loss to Baylor and tossed 5 touchdowns in a win at home against Iowa State. Then in a game that got the Raiders bowl eligible, he threw for 384 yards and 3 touchdowns in a win against Kansas State.[xix]

In the last game of 2015, Mahomes faced Texas, one of the team's biggest rivals. The Raiders had not won in Austin since 1998 on Thanksgiving. However, with Mahomes and Texas having a down year, they felt like they may have been able to break that slump.[xviii]

After a quiet first three quarters, Mahomes began making plays with his arm and legs. He led the Red Raiders to 21 fourth-quarter points, throwing and rushing for a touchdown, in helping lead his team to their first win in almost 20 years in Austin against Texas. It was indeed an incredible moment for the team as the Red Raiders ended the year 7-5.[xvii]

The Red Raiders finished the year in the New Orleans Bowl against Louisiana Tech. It would not be Mahomes' last time playing in an NFL stadium. Despite losing, Mahomes shined, passing 4 touchdowns and throwing for 370 yards. Mahomes ended the year throwing for 4,563 yards and 36 touchdowns. He was fourth in total yards and sixth in touchdowns across all of college football.[xix]

By the end of his junior season, Mahomes felt like he had more in him. He wanted to be a starting NFL quarterback. He worked hard in the offseason to perfect his game and strengthen his accuracy and consistency. He spent a lot of time with Kingsbury and his wide receivers. It would pay off when 2016 came around.

NFL teams began to look at Mahomes in the event he would leave Texas Tech after his junior season, but there were still a lot of question marks concerning his unique throwing style and speculation about whether or not his technique would work in the NFL. Many Texas Tech quarterbacks in the past had also been successful in the high dynamic offense but it did not equate to the pro level. Kingsbury was one of them.

There was also the conference they were in. Many NFL scouts overlook a lot of the Big 12 quarterbacks because the defenses are weaker than most other power 5 conferences. Teams like Texas Tech, Kansas,

Oklahoma State, Baylor, and Kansas State are more offensive-oriented and not known for playing good defense.

For Mahomes, his junior season would be one of the best any college quarterback had ever had. After throwing for 483 yards in the opening game against Stephen F. Austin State, the Red Raiders traveled to Arizona State. Mahomes went 38-for-53 for 540 yards, also tossing 2 touchdowns. Unfortunately, in what would be a common theme that season, the Red Raiders gave up 9 touchdowns, losing 68-55.[xix]

The following week against Louisiana Tech, Mahomes threw for five touchdowns followed by four against Kansas. Then it was another 500-yard performance against Kansas State. Through five games that season, Mahomes had already thrown for more than 2,300 yards with 20 touchdowns, outperforming all other quarterbacks in college.[xix]

One of Mahomes' greatest college games came against Oklahoma on Oct. 22, 2016. The 16th-ranked Sooners traveled to Lubbock behind the arm of Baker Mayfield and it was destined to be a shootout. It certainly was and turned out to be one of the best football games of the 2016 college football season. Both Mayfield and Mahomes were gunslinging it all over the place, but Mahomes was more of the story. He tore apart the Sooners defense, beating them over the top numerous times. Mahomes' final stat line was an incredible 52-for-88 for 734 yards and 5 touchdowns. As if throwing for five touchdowns was not enough, he also ran for two against the Sooners defense. Mahomes tied for the most passing yards in a Division I game and he set the all-time record for most all-purpose yards (passing and rushing) as he compiled 819 yards—and all this while battling a sprained AC joint in his throwing shoulder.[xvii]

It caught the attention of media members everywhere, including NFL scouts. Despite losing 66-59, it was one of the more memorable games ever at Lubbock Stadium.

As the season neared its close, it was believed Mahomes was going to leave Texas Tech early and enter the NFL Draft. By the time the Baylor game came around the final week of the season, NFL scouts were paying full attention to him. Mahomes would give Texas Tech fans, and NFL scouts, one final showcase before he left the school.

Playing at Cowboys Stadium in Arlington against their rival Baylor, Mahomes led the Raiders to a 54-35 victory to close out the season and his college career. It was one of Mahomes' best. He threw for 586 yards and 6 touchdowns.[xvii]

That season, Mahomes led all of college football with 5,052 passing yards, ranking him No. 14 all-time for most passing yards in a season. Mahomes was third in college football with 41 touchdowns and was second in total completions (388).[xix]

In just two seasons, Mahomes had thrown for over 9,700 yards as a Red Raider and accounted for 99 touchdowns. On Jan. 3, 2017 he made it official. He was entering the NFL Draft.

"I want to thank Texas Tech for teaching me to be a fearless champion, athletically and academically," Mahomes said in a message that he posted. "Thank you to the fans for their continued support, through the good times and the bad. They made me love this university."[xix]

Mahomes' skill was just part of the legacy he was leaving at Texas Tech. He was also a true leader and a positive influence on those around them. He engaged with the fans, realizing their passion for Red Raider football and wanting to give them something to cheer about. He always carried a positive attitude with him and a smile whenever he was on the field or the sideline. He had gained the respect of his teammates and coaches.[xix]

Kingsbury knew, though, this was not the end.

"It was tough to lose him, but I knew when he went into that draft, he was going to be an NFL star. There was not a doubt in my mind."[xvii]

Chapter 4: NFL Career

The Draft

Patrick Mahomes was projected to be a second-round acquisition according to early ratings given to him by NFL scouts. He had the opportunity to raise that rating, however, through the Combine and team workouts.

Mahomes did just that. Mahomes traveled to Indianapolis for Pro Day at the NFL Combine to showcase his skills along with hundreds of other college athletes. It was an opportunity for players entering the draft to demonstrate their talents in front of coaches and scouts from all 32 NFL teams. This played a major role in a player's draft stock. They would go through all sorts of drills and simulated workouts and then schedule individual team workouts if there was interest. They would also run the 40-yard dash and take all sorts of physical and mental tests.

It did not take long for scouts to be impressed with Mahomes. In his simulated workouts, he made a series of throws that left coaches and scouts' mouths open.

"When his workout ended, everyone applauded," Wes Welker said, who at the time was working with the Houston Texans coaching staff. "I was like, 'Man, do people normally applaud at a pro day?' One of the scouts was like, 'I've been a scout for 30-plus years. I've never seen everybody applaud after a workout.'"[xx]

Mahomes had always been that under-the radar-guy in football. Once again, he was doing things no one else had seen. This was who he was, though—the guy who wanted to go above and beyond expectations. And the quotes from scouts proved he was accomplishing just that.

As if the workout was not already great, Mahomes finished with a flourish. On his final throw during a simulated scrimmage, he threw an 80-yard Hail Mary on the button for a touchdown.

"I'd never seen anything like it in my life," Welker said. "It was like, 'Did that just happen'?"[xx]

Mahomes' family and college and high school coaches were not surprised, though. In fact, they were more taken aback by people being surprised at what they were witnessing. His old coaches and family had already witnessed this in front of their own eyes before. They already knew what he was capable of.

What made Mahomes' workout even more impressive was that he took on throws that most quarterbacks shy away from, even the pros. He was throwing 20-yard comeback routes between the cornerback and safety. It was a risky thing to do in a combine because it could hurt your draft position if it failed, but Mahomes was right on the mark with every throw. The arm strength, velocity, and most importantly, the accuracy impressed everyone.[xx]

Many general managers were in attendance, but the Kansas City Chiefs general manager, Brett Veach, was not. Veach said that he already saw what he needed to see out of Mahomes. After watching tape on him at Pro Day, it only confirmed to Veach that he was the real deal. Veach wanted him badly, and when he heard about the workout, the only concern was that they would have to give up a lot to move from the 27th pick in the first round to get him. Mahomes stock was understandably rising.[xx]

Draft experts like Mel Kiper and Todd McShay moved Mahomes up in their rankings and projected him to be a late first-round pick. However, many felt he could drop all the way to the third round. Many times, NFL quarterbacks drop because teams are already settled with their future. Aaron Rodgers went from being a top-5 projected pick to No. 24. Ben Roethlisberger expected to be drafted within the first few picks but sat there until No. 11. Dan Marino slid all the way to No. 27 with five quarterbacks picked ahead of him.

There were also many lingering questions on Mahomes. The biggest one was whether his unique style would translate to the NFL. Everyone knew by now that he did not grow up a quarterback. He was a baseball player that converted to football during high school. These kinds of stories do not usually translate into pro bowl quarterbacks. There was also the fact he played at Texas Tech, not a school known for grooming NFL quarterbacks because of the offense they play. It is much more wide open as you operate against weaker defenses from the Big 12. The NFL is a much tougher experience with tighter windows to throw through.[xxi]

As draft day approached, Mahomes declined to attend the NFL Draft in Philadelphia. Instead, he stayed home and rented a room at a country club in Tyler, Texas where his parents and agent Leigh Steinberg were in attendance. One of the reasons that many felt Mahomes did not want to attend was that he was concerned he would drop—and he had already seen Aaron Rodgers and more recently, quarterback Brady Quinn, just sit there uncomfortably and wait with the cameras pinned on them the whole time. It was not a good scene. He preferred to stay away from the drama in Philadelphia should he not be selected early.

Steinberg, however, felt confident Mahomes would not wait long. In fact, in talks with other teams, he felt he would go within the first 10 to 15 picks. Plus, he knew there was one team in particular that would stop a fall from happening should it start.

"The draft is less mysterious when one is representing a player than it is known to the general public," Steinberg said. "The Chiefs expressed interest to us early in the process, and we knew they really liked

Patrick. But they were going to have to move up several spots if they were going to make it happen."[xxi]

Many times if you like a player so much but are concerned he is not going to make it to your pick, you need to put together a package of draft picks to rise up and get that player. The more you move up, the more you have to give away. If the Chiefs thought Mahomes was going to go in the first 15 picks, they were going to give away at least a first-round draft pick to move up that high from number 27.

Clark Hunt was the owner of the Kansas City Chiefs and was admittedly nervous about drafting Mahomes. He had seen other journeyman quarterbacks fail far too often. But he knew Veach was in love with him and head coach Andy Reid also had grown to appreciate his skills and wanted him to be drafted.

As the draft began, the Chiefs felt a growing sense of doubt that Mahomes would not make it all the way until their draft pick. However, after spending the day on the phone with other general managers, Veach had it set up that if Mahomes fell to No. 10, they would make a move. After nine picks, Mahomes was not yet selected. The Chiefs had negotiated with the Buffalo Bills and pulled the trigger on a trade that was discussed, sending Buffalo their No. 27 pick, their third-round pick, and their 2018 first-round pick for the right to move up to No. 10. And with that pick, they took Mahomes.[xxi]

"I couldn't tell you how ecstatic we were that he was there," Veach said. "We were nervous that he wouldn't drop that far, but when he fell to No. 10, we wanted to try and move ahead of other teams and get him before it was too late."[xxi]

It was the right move. Houston moved up to select Deshaun Watson two picks later, but it is unclear whether they would have taken Mahomes over Watson had he dropped to 12. Many of the scouts on Houston were in love with Mahomes, a Texas prodigy, and despite post-draft talk that said they (the Texans) wanted Watson all along, no one truly knew.[xxi]

One thing was clear: Mahomes was now a Kansas City Chief.

Everybody liked this guy," Reid said. "We couldn't find anybody that didn't like him. I thought Willie [Davis] did a great job of scouting him. We got to know the kid before we got to know the kid. Everybody kind of just fell in love with the kid and what he was all about and how he went about his business and how he played. That does not happen every year. I'm saying it like it's easy. That's not something that happens every year. When that happens, Ron Wolf told me this a long time ago: 'If you have one of those guys that you like, you go get them.'"[xxi]

For Andy Reid to say that meant a lot. Reid knew quarterbacks well and was a great quarterback coach. He worked with and elevated the game of Brett Favre, he groomed Donovan McNabb from his rookie days and turned Alex Smith from an average quarterback into a Pro Bowler. With Reid on board, there was growing confidence the pick was the right one.

Rookie Season

"He (Alex Smith) was extremely important. The way he went about his business and being a pro's pro, a great quarterback, and also a great human being. He taught me a ton of just the process and how to blueprint your week and how to game plan. He helped me out a lot in the early part of my career, even still to this day of being able to get those invaluable lessons from him."[xxii] - Patrick Mahomes

All rookie quarterbacks that are taken in the first and second rounds are handled differently. Some head coaches want to throw them out there right away into the action and start on day one, as was the case with Andrew Luck, Alex Smith, Ben Roethlisberger, and Eli Manning. Other coaches want them to sit several games and even a full season learning behind a veteran quarterback and easing them into action. This helped quarterbacks like Philip Rivers, Aaron Rodgers, and Carson Palmer develop greatly for when they finally did step into the starting role.

Andy Reid felt the latter would best help Mahomes in the long run, especially behind a guy like Alex Smith who was once a first-round pick with the 49ers and had veteran experience. Smith knew Mahomes was the future. You do not give up a first-round pick and move up 17 spots to let a guy sit for several years or be a career backup behind you. He knew his time in Kansas City was limited. Reid knew it would not be easy on Alex, but it was because of how Alex handled the situation that made Mahomes a better player.

"Alex Smith was phenomenal," Reid said. "He wasn't asked to do this, but he let Patrick into his world. Patrick handled it the right way. He was humbled around Alex. He didn't try to overstep his bounds with Alex when he competed. With that, Alex let him kind of tag along on the field and off the field, showed him how to be a pro. How to study, your diet, your workout plan, family, how you work your family into the National Football League to be a great player in the National Football League. I joke about it, but it's true. Patrick couldn't pay Alex enough for what he gave him with the experience."[xxii]

It was not easy for Mahomes, either. He had the desire to get out there and play right away. He was a competitor, so sitting on the sidelines watching almost the entire first season play out in front of him had to be driving him crazy inside, but instead of letting it get to him, he looked at the other aspect of it: learning.

"I attribute a lot of my early success to Alex," Mahomes said. "He showed me how to be both a great football player and human being at the same time. He worked with me and took me under his wing and I will forever appreciate that."[xxiii]

A great mentor means a lot. After all, would Aaron Rodgers be as good without the mentorship of the legendary Brett Favre? How about Phillip Rivers, if he was not learning from Drew Brees? The best example may even be Steve Young who was mentored by Joe Montana.

Mahomes got a chance to play in the preseason with the second-stringers and made his presence known right away. Fans were impressed by the strength of his arm and the throws he was making. While many do not take preseason games very seriously and how guys look, it was quite impressive and led to some early optimism for Mahomes amongst all Chiefs fans. His throws were just as impressive with the Chiefs as they were at Texas Tech. Once the season started, however, Mahomes was back on the bench, playing with the second team in practice.

Every day at practice, running back coach Eric Bieniemy said Mahomes and Smith were always side by side. They had a great relationship as teacher and student. Smith constantly worked with Mahomes and was a role model to him, even staying after practice to help him improve in all aspects. What made it special is both men had a very positive attitude.[xxiii]

Winning helped also. While helping Mahomes develop, Smith was also helping his team win the AFC West on the field. After a 29-13 win over the Miami Dolphins in Week 16, the Chiefs had clinched their division and were set to play in the postseason. In a unique position, the Chiefs Week 17 game against the Denver Broncos would not affect their playoff seeding. They were locked into the 4th spot. Reid thought it best to sit his starters who would have to play the following week in the Wild Card round. That meant sitting Smith and giving Patrick Mahomes his first-ever career start, a road game against the Denver Broncos.

Mahomes would play with the second-stringers that he practiced with in his first game going up against the starting Broncos defense on a frigid 17-degree day in Denver. The first throw he ever made in the NFL (regular season) was an early indication of how his career would pan out. On third-and-10 and lining up in the shotgun, Mahomes slung a missile in between a tight window of two defenders to Demetrius Harris for a 51-yard gain.[xxiv]

Not a bad start to your career.

For anyone who said his college-style would not equate to the more difficult defenses in the pros, they were already starting to eat their words.

"That pass told you everything you needed to know about him," Chiefs guard Laurent Duvernay-Tardif said. "We knew he had a big arm and that he wasn't afraid to use it. But it's one thing to make that throw in practice and another to make it in a game situation. He delivered."[xxiv]

Teammates like Duvernay-Tardif gained a newfound respect for him from then on. They saw him in a different light and were reassured this was the future of Kansas City football.

In the end, Mahomes finished with 22 completions in 35 attempts while throwing for 284 yards and no touchdowns. The media was gushing about Mahomes' performance. ESPN analyst Louis Riddick called the performance "ridiculous," saying the man showed no fear and could make any throw he wanted. He could "still get it done even when things weren't perfect."[xxiv]

The Chiefs ended that season 10-6 but lost at home in the first round of the Wild Card against the Titans. The Chiefs led 21-3 at halftime and were helped out by incredible quarterback play from Alex Smith, but the second half saw Marcus Mariota and Derrick Henry take over while the Chiefs offense were stuck in neutral. The Titans rallied to win 22-21, ending the Chiefs season. It also was the last game for Alex Smith in a Chiefs uniform. Shortly after the Super Bowl, the Chiefs traded him to the Redskins.

It was Mahomes' team now. And things would only get better from then on.

MVP Season

"The way he started his career, it's unlike any other in NFL history."[xxv] - Trent Green, ESPN analyst.

Mahomes entered his second season as the clear number one guy in Kansas City. After a great final game of the 2017 season against the Broncos, there were high expectations that Mahomes would be a Pro Bowl quarterback and more. They just did not expect greatness to come as quickly as it did.

Mahomes took the team under his wing from the start. In training camp, he established himself as a leader right away, taking over right where Alex Smith had left off. It did not take long for players to gain considerable respect for him and he instantly built a rapport with wide receivers Tyreek Hill and Travis Kelce. By preseason, the team knew something the rest of the NFL did not: they could win a Super Bowl with this guy sooner rather than later. They could not wait for their quarterback to show the rest of the NFL how good he was.

The season started with a splash. After a four-touchdown performance and win to start the season in Los Angeles against the Chargers, Mahomes traveled to Pittsburgh. It was perhaps this game that caught everyone's attention.

The Chiefs offense torched the much-vaunted Steelers defense. Mahomes threw 6 touchdown passes and went 23-for-28 for 328 yards in leading the Chiefs to a 42-37 win at Heinz Field. Mike Tomlin said he was mesmerized by the second-year quarterback, saying he threw everything at him and he just kept throwing the ball over his defense. The 10 touchdowns in his first two games set an all-time record for most touchdown passes thrown in the first two games of the season. Mahomes also became the second Chiefs quarterback in history to throw for six or more touchdowns in his first two games.[xxvii]

And the records would not stop there.

Mahomes went on a string of 300-plus yard games that went all the way into November. One of his best moments came on a Monday night game against the Broncos where he made an incredible escape from NFL Defensive Player of the Year Vonn Miller and then threw the ball left-handed for a spectacular completion, keeping a drive alive with his team down by three late in the game. The throw stunned announcer Jon Gruden who compared what he was watching from Mahomes to that of Brett Favre, whom he had coached back in the early 1990s in Green Bay. Mahomes continued the drive and led the team to a game-winning touchdown on the road and a 4-0 start.[xxvii]

After a 5-0 start, the Chiefs were headed to New England for an epic Sunday night game that lived up to its hype and more. In a clash with Tom Brady, the two put on performances that would lead it to become one of the greatest games of the 2018 NFL season. Down 40-33 with three minutes left and backed up to their own 25, Mahomes threw a laser down the field on the button to Tyreek Hill, who used his speed to outrace the Patriots defenders down the sidelines and tie the game at 40. It was Mahomes' fourth touchdown of the game, but unfortunately, their defense could not stop Brady and the Patriots from going down the field to kick a game-winning field goal to win 43-40. It would not be Mahomes and Brady's last epic battle that year, however.[xxvii]

Through 10 games of the season, the Chiefs were 9-1 and had the best record in the NFL, along with the Los Angeles Rams. Mahomes had thrown 31 touchdowns, the most through the first games of an NFL season. Half of his games included four or more touchdown passes in a game. He had just two games where he failed to eclipse 300 yards.[xxxix]

A classic Monday night game awaited between the 9-1 Chiefs and the 9-1 Rams. The game, which was supposed to be held in Mexico City, was moved to Los Angeles because of stadium concerns in Mexico. Fans expected a shootout between Mahomes and Jared Goff and they got it. If the earlier Patriots and Chiefs game was *one* of the best of the 2018 season, the Chiefs-Rams contest was likely the best.

Both offenses showcased their talent. Mahomes bulldozed over the Rams defense, throwing for 478 yards and 6 touchdowns. Goff threw for 4 touchdowns and 379 yards and was able to keep up with the Chiefs scoring. In the end, despite Mahomes being the star of the game and setting an NFL record with 37 touchdowns through six games, the Rams outlasted the Chiefs in a classic thriller, 54-51.[xxvii]

As the weather got colder and the year wound down, Mahomes numbers dropped some in the terms of yardage but he was still throwing touchdowns. He helped lead the Chiefs to 12 wins, their most wins in 15 years, and helped secure home-field advantage throughout the playoffs. Mahomes threw for 5,029 yards and led the league with an astounding 50 touchdowns and yards per pass attempt (9.58). The 50 touchdowns shattered Len Dawson's record of 30 touchdowns in a season by a Kansas City Chiefs player. Mahomes also broke Trent Green's record for most passing yards in a season by a Chiefs player and most passing yards and touchdowns through a player's first 16 career starts.[xxviii]

Mahomes' performance led him to being awarded the 2018 NFL Offensive Most Valuable Player. In the NFL playoffs, while Mahomes was optimistic he could lead his team to the Super Bowl, Chiefs fans were nervous. They had seen this song and dance play out before. They were notorious for flaming out in the playoffs and had a head coach who had a great regular-season record but had only been to one Super Bowl—which he had lost as head coach of the Philadelphia

Eagles. Unfortunately, Reid had the reputation of not being a great playoff coach.

The previous season, the Chiefs won the division and lost in the Wild Card round. In 2016, they finished 12-4 but lost to the Steelers in the Divisional round. The Chiefs even had two 13-3 seasons in 1995 and 1997 and still lost their opening playoff games in the Divisional round. All in all, the Chiefs were 1-9 in their last 10 playoff appearances. They had not been to the Super Bowl since 1969, their only Super Bowl appearance which they happened to win.[xxxix]

Their opening divisional round game came against Andrew Luck and the Colts. Right from the start, Mahomes calmed Chiefs' fans nerves and made them realize this was not the Chiefs of old. He led them down the field to two scores in the first quarter and had them up 24-7 at halftime. The Chiefs dominated the Colts and got great play from their defense as well. In the end, Mahomes went 27-for-41 throwing for 278 yards. The Chiefs won 31-13 to advance to the AFC Championship Game against the five-time Super Bowl-champion New England Patriots, the same team that had beat them in a classic 43-40 shootout earlier in the season.[xxvii]

A lot of hype surrounded Kansas City that week as the Patriots came to town. Could Andy Reid and Patrick Mahomes take out the formidable Pats and propel their offense to the Super Bowl?

The AFC Championship was played on a cold night in Kansas City with the kickoff temperature under 20 degrees. The frigid weather took its toll as both offenses started off slowly. And at halftime, both Brady and Mahomes were nowhere near the quarterbacks they were in Week 6 when they were throwing touchdowns left and right. But Brady used his experience to conjure up enough plays to get the Patriots some points before halftime while Mahomes could not get anything going. The Chiefs trailed 14-0 midway through the game and 17-7 through three quarters.[xxvii]

But in the fourth quarter, Mahomes came alive. He found weaknesses in the Patriots defense and began making big plays. He threw two touchdown passes to Damien Williams to give the Chiefs the lead. Back and forth the teams went in the fourth quarter, both teams suddenly warmed up and gutting the opposing defense. Brady and Mahomes once again looked like the quarterbacks they had been all season.

The Patriots put together a late drive and appeared to have won the game with a Rex Burkhead 4-yard run, which gave the Patriots a 31-28 lead with only 39 seconds left on the clock. But that 39 seconds was all Mahomes needed; he made two big throws down the field to set up a game-tying field goal at the end of the game—and just like that, they were knotted at 31 and headed into overtime.[xxvii]

The Patriots got the ball first and then the unthinkable happened—Tom Brady was suddenly picked off deep in his own end. The Chiefs began to celebrate, believing they were likely on their way to the Super Bowl. Mahomes grabbed his helmet, ready to set the team up in game-winning field goal territory.

But not so fast. There was a flag.

Dee Ford, not even a factor in the play, was lined up offsides at the snap. Replays showed it was very close, but the call gave the ball back to the Patriots and, sadly, the Chiefs would never see it again. After all, there is a reason why Tom Brady is Tom Brady. Putting on the kind of show he was legendary for, he took the Patriots right down the field and then handed it off to Burkhead on the last play of the drive, who proceeded to run it in from two yards, landing the final blow and ripping out the hearts of all Chiefs fans and players at Arrowhead Stadium that night.[xxvii]

"That was tough," Mahomes said. "Especially not to even get a chance to get the ball in overtime. But we fought hard and came back. There will be more opportunities to come."[xxvi]

Mahomes must have found it difficult to stay positive like that after such a disappointing loss, but he had been that way his whole career. He always tried to find the positive side out of the negative. He knew there was a promising future ahead for the Chiefs. Indeed, the team had made great strides that season and he knew without a doubt that they were only going to get better.

The NFL's Offensive MVP finished the season with some very impressive achievements and broke many team records with NFL records starting to pile up as well. Mahomes' star was shining brightly as the Chiefs steamrolled into the 2019 season. It would be a rollercoaster ride even more thrilling than 2018 was— and with a much happier ending.

"Super" Mahomes

If there was one thing that Patrick Mahomes has learned throughout his life, it is that there is always room to grow. Keep getting better. Push to be the best and have the attitude to win. Despite a crushing loss in the AFC Championship in 2018, Mahomes kept a positive attitude and drove to improve his play, even after an MVP season.

Mahomes was a competitor and he kept his teammates positive in the offseason, motivating them to get better and take the next step as a team. They made great gains in 2018 and it was time to take the next step in 2019.

Mahomes began the 2019 season right where he left off. Just when some thought he might take a step back in 2019 after an incredible 2018, he quickly proved his doubters wrong.

Going up against the vaunted Jaguars defense in the Florida heat, Mahomes had a field day throwing all over the field and piling up big play after play. Despite losing his top wide receiver, Tyreek Hill, to a leg injury, Mahomes stayed on top of his game. He went 25-for-33 for 378 yards and 3 touchdowns in a 40-26 opening day win.[xxxix]

The next week in Oakland, he was even better. He found Sammy Watkins deep twice in the game and threw for 443 yards against the Raiders with 4 touchdowns to lead his team to another win. The following week he was 27-for-37 for 374 yards against the great Ravens defense, throwing for 3 more touchdowns. He looked like he would easily win another NFL MVP at this rate.[xxxix]

Mahomes, however, tweaked his ankle in a Sunday night game against the Colts in Week 5. It affected his ability to scramble. Even worse, the rest of his team was getting hurt. Hill was already out and Sammy Watkins was the next to exit with an injury. Offensive linemen were also going down, and by the second half of the game, Mahomes was running out of players to throw to when Travis Kelce was sidelined. Defensively, they were also losing bodies and were being gashed by the Colts running backs. It was just too much to overcome and the Chiefs lost their first game of the season, following with another loss the following week at home to Houston. Mahomes was clearly off his game with his hobbling ankle, despite throwing for three touchdowns against the Texans.[xxxix]

Then against Denver on a Thursday night game, Mahomes went for a quarterback sneak and got his ankle piled on early in the game. He left the game with a dislocated ankle that would likely cost him one to two months of downtime and put the Chiefs playoff hopes in jeopardy. He was replaced by veteran Matt Moore.

Mahomes, however, kept his positive attitude, and instead of getting down, he went right to work rehabbing the ankle. He worked hard to strengthen it as much as possible, and within two weeks, he was already well ahead of schedule an eying an early return. Reid was cautious, not wanting to rush him back, but did activate him to start after missing just three games. In his first game back, Mahomes was back to peak form and had his favorite target Tyreek Hill back as well. Mahomes went 36-for-50 for 446 yards but lost in a shootout to the Titans 35-32.[xxxix]

Mahomes was shattering records. He broke Kurt Warner's record for most passing yards in a quarterback's first 25 starts with 8,007 yards. He also passed legendary quarterback Dan Marino with 68 touchdown tosses in his first 25 games. Additionally, he compiled the highest passer rating and most completions of any quarterback in history through their first 25 games.[xxix]

As great as these records were, Mahomes still had one particular goal on his mind that season: A Super Bowl ring.

The Chiefs finished 12-4 for the second straight season, and thanks to an uncharacteristic late-season collapse by the Patriots, the Chiefs clinched home-field advantage for the second straight season. Even more stunning was New England's Wild Card loss at home to the Tennessee Titans, which ended the hopes of a Brady-Mahomes AFC Championship rematch. It was also the end of Brady's career in New England as he would leave for Tampa Bay in the following offseason.

In the Chiefs' AFC Division Round game against the Texans, they got off to a devastating start. It appeared after the first quarter that the Chiefs 12-4 season would be for naught. The Texans seemed unstoppable, and with just 10 minutes left until halftime, the Chiefs found themselves down 24-0 and their season was suddenly on life support. They were playing so poorly, the fans at Arrowhead Stadium were actually booing them.[xxx]

But Mahomes' positive attitude paid dividends as he kept his team's spirits up, never letting them get down. He would not let them give in to desperation, rather he kept them calm. He told them not to panic and that they had it in them to come back and win the game. The team rallied around Mahomes' leadership, and from that point on in the game, it was like a completely different Chiefs team.

It started with a 17-yard touchdown pass to Damien Williams. 24-7. Then Mahomes led them down the field again and threw a touchdown to Travis Kelce. 24-14. Then after a turnover, the Chiefs converted it into more points when Mahomes hit Kelce for a short touchdown pass. 24-21. Finally, back on their own 10-yard line, Mahomes carved up the Texans defense with his arms and legs and took them 90 yards down the field before halftime, ending it with another touchdown pass to Kelce. By halftime and in the span of just 10 minutes, the Chiefs had completed a breathtaking comeback and already had a 28-24 lead.[xxx]

But they were not finished. Mahomes led them on two long drives to begin the third quarter, one for 77 yards and another for 85 yards to break the game wide open. When all was said and done, Mahomes had one of the best games of his career, going 23-for-35 for 321 yards and throwing 5 touchdowns. He also led the team in rushing with 53 yards on the ground. The Chiefs were advancing to the AFC Championship with a 51-31 win over Houston.[xxx]

The Tennessee Titans awaited them, who were the surprise opponent after they had stunned both the Super Bowl-champion Patriots and then the AFC's top-seeded Ravens. The Titans were led by Derrick Henry, the NFL's top rusher that season. It foreshadowed a difficult battle to come, especially since the Chiefs' run defense was considered a weakness and many thought the Titans could exploit that perceived vulnerability and advance to the Super Bowl.

Like the game against Houston, the Chiefs got off to a slow start and trailed 10-7 through one quarter. But once again, Mahomes rallied the team on his back and made plays when he needed to. Down 17-7 with under five minutes to go until halftime, Mahomes threw a perfect pass to Tyreek Hill for a touchdown. Then after a defensive stop, Mahomes took his team down the field from their 14-yard line. With just 11 seconds left, Mahomes scrambled to his left and saw a lane down the sideline and took it. He scampered 27 yards and into the end zone, sending the fans into a frenzy and giving the Chiefs their first lead of the day.[xxxi]

The Chiefs controlled the second half and Mahomes continued to make plays. A picture-perfect 60-yard pass landed in the hands of Sammy Watkins, who took it in for a touchdown to break the game open. The Chiefs won 35-24 and were on their way to Super

Bowl LIV to face the San Francisco 49ers, who later that day had beaten the Green Bay Packers.[xxxi]

"I mean, it's amazing. It really is," said Mahomes, who had three touchdowns in the game. "To be here, to be a part of Chiefs Kingdom and to be able to do it here at Arrowhead, these people deserve it. And we're not done yet."[xxxi]

That Chiefs Kingdom was worshipping Mahomes perhaps more than any other player in their history, perhaps even more than Lenny Dawson or Joe Montana. It had been a long time since they had a player with such charisma who also gave them hope for a great future. This was just the beginning.

Mahomes and his team would travel to Miami for the Super Bowl against a 49ers team that was number two in the NFL in total defense. It would not be as easy as it had been against the Texans and Titans.

Leading up to the Super Bowl, all the talk was on Mahomes and his quick adaptability to flourish in the

NFL. And people were catching on to what a great a story this was—a kid who did not play quarterback until his second year in high school. This was less than 10 years ago! There are not many athletes who can begin a sport and become so great in such a short span of time. Tiger Woods started playing golf at the age of three. Tom Brady was holding a football at four. Lionel Messi was juggling a soccer ball at five. And Mahomes? He was holding baseballs and basketballs at that point, not footballs. Yet suddenly here he was, wowing the NFL world with his unorthodox style and spectacular achievements. It was unfathomable as much as it was exciting. And what a phenomenally great narrative it was, indeed.

But the Super Bowl would not be a given by any means. The 49ers would make life hard for Mahomes. They had a stout defensive line led by Nick Bosa. In fact, the Niners were literally the best team in the NFL against the pass at the time and were third in sacks.

Mahomes certainly had his work cut out for him and then some.

For three-and-a-half quarters of the Super Bowl, it looked as if the 49ers defense had found the Chiefs' kryptonite. And for the first time in his career, Mahomes seemed perplexed out there. The masterful pressure poured on by the 49ers' defense was getting to him. He had thrown two picks. He had just 172 passing yards and it appeared he might have his first full game of his NFL career with under 200 passing yards in a game. Despite running for a score, he had thrown zero touchdowns. His 5.9-yard completion rate was 3 yards less than his career average. His 49.2 quarterback rating was also the worst he ever had this deep into a game. Worse yet, his team was down 20-10. After a Mahomes interception, the 49ers had the ball and were looking to put the final nail in the coffin.[xxxii]

But Mahomes did not panic. He had been there before. They were down against Houston and came back.

They were down against Tennessee and came back. Yes, coming back when down by 10 against the 49ers in the Super Bowl would be a little tougher, but Mahomes stayed calm and knew he could do it. He knew he could lead his team back to win the Lombardi Trophy.

Heroes make the best of their opportunities. It came on an incredible third-and-15 at their own 35. With seven minutes left, the game likely on the line, and Mahomes facing pressure, he launched a deep throw down the field to an open Tyreek Hill, who made the catch and advanced to the 49ers' 20-yard line. It was the play that changed all the momentum in the game. After a pass interference call in the end zone put the ball on the 1-yard line, Mahomes found Kelce in the back of the end zone to bring the Chiefs within 3 points.[xxxii]

After the Chiefs' defense came through again and forced a punt, Mahomes marched his team right down the field again, making crisp passes and looking remarkably poised under the unrelenting pressure. On a big third down at the 49ers' 5-yard line, Mahomes hit running back Damien Williams on a screen pass that took him into the end zone to give the Chiefs the lead. After not throwing a touchdown for 53 minutes, Mahomes threw two of them in just three minutes.[xxxii]

The Chiefs defense would come through again and stop the Niners on a crucial 4th down with 1:25 left. When taking over, Williams broke free down the sidelines and ran in for a touchdown. It was now 31-20 and the Chiefs sideline began to celebrate. They had done the incredible.[xxxii]

The stat line at the end would not suggest that Mahomes had his greatest game, but it is not always all about stats. It is about leadership and coming through at the time it is needed most. Over those final three drives, Mahomes was 8-for-12 for 112 yards with 2 touchdowns and a 130.2 passer rating. Mahomes proved that he was the special athlete he was hyped up to be as he unflinchingly led his team to their first Super Bowl in 50 years. Mahomes was named the game's Most Valuable Player. He was also the youngest player in history, at 24 years old, to be named NFL MVP and Super Bowl MVP in their career.[xxxii]

Mahomes was humble in his post-game speech, crediting the defense for giving him the opportunity to get the ball back three times to score after he had not been playing well. He also credited his offensive line, who, despite struggling to keep the defensive line away from him, had given him time in the fourth quarter and opened up holes for Williams.

"I feel like, even if something goes wrong, I have confidence in my team and they'll fix it," Mahomes said.[xxxiii]

His team had done just that. In three games, the Chiefs found ways to come back and make history. He put his faith in himself, the guys around him, and his coach, and he left Miami as a Super Bowl champion with more greatness to come in the future.

Chapter 5: Personal Life

Love Life

Unlike some athletes, Mahomes found the love of his life early. During his sophomore year in high school, he met Brittany Matthews, who happened to also be an athlete at the time.

Matthews played soccer in high school and then went on to play college soccer for the University of Texas at Tyler and then for UMF Afturelding in Europe. There, she spent much of her time playing in Iceland. After that, she opened her own fitness company and became a personal trainer. While she did not grow up a Chiefs fan, she came to love them when Patrick signed with the team in 2017 and has been to almost all of his games. She currently runs the website Brittany Lynne Fitness. [xxxv]

Her experience in sports, particularly playing professionally in Europe, has helped Mahomes a lot since they have been together. She has helped Mahomes with his overall fitness as well and played an integral part in him healing his ankle after he dislocated it in 2019.

Mahomes has gotten so much support from his girlfriend, who shares a similar positive attitude. Mahomes has said it played a major role in his success early in his career. Despite having a long-distance relationship in college, they remained extremely close and encouraged each other to become better athletes.

The two of them recently purchased a house in Kansas City worth just under $2 million. They shared the video of their home on social media and proclaimed their love for the city.

"Setting down roots in Kansas City was huge for us. I think the people are what we love the most about

Kansas City," Mahomes said. "We're trying to be here for a long, long time."[xxxiv]

It is important to have that connection with your city and to feel comfortable there. There is nothing worse than playing in a city where you aren't happy. Living in Kansas City, a city both Patrick and Brittany love, has only made life more enjoyable and kept them happy.

The youthful couple may not be parents to a child yet, but they are in love with their dogs, which they adopted in 2017 and 2019, Steel and Silver. The two of them regularly post photos of themselves with their pooches on social media. If you ever get on Instagram, you'll see the obsession of Patrick and Brittany with Steel and Silver.[xxxv]

Hobbies

Patrick enjoyed baseball (a career path he seriously considered until ultimately deciding on football), basketball, ping pong, and many other sports and competitive games. And one of Patrick's biggest hobbies besides hanging out with his dogs is playing golf. Patrick grew up playing it and actually thought about making a career of golf when he was younger.

"I really tried to get into golf. My dad played so it's something else I compete against him in. He is definitely better, but I did beat him when he came to Kansas City one time. That was my only time I've ever beat him though."[xxxv]

Every athlete needs that distraction or hobby on the side to take the pressure off your regular job. For Patrick, it was golf. It was fun for him. He is competitive with it, even against his dad.[xxxv]

Mahomes also spends a lot of his time helping with his charity, the 15 and the Mahomies Foundation, which he established in 2019. The mission of the foundation is to "improve the lives of children and support initiatives that focus on health, wellness, communities in need of resources and other charitable causes."[xxxvi]

Mahomes spends a lot of time trying to lift the spirits of children that are in the foundation. He calls it one of his favorite hobbies because he gets to make a positive impact in the lives of children who need it most.

Recently, Mahomes made a visit to Children's Mercy Hospital where he surprised the children with gifts. He brought PlayStations, robots, toys, and clothes and spent the day bringing smiles to their faces.[xxxvi]

Mahomes currently carries a net worth of $30 million and just recently signed a 10-year extension with the Chiefs worth over $500 million, passing Russell Wilson as the NFL's highest-paid player. He currently has endorsement deals with Essentia Water, Hy-Vee Grocery Stores, Oakley Eyewear, and Adidas. Additionally, he has a deal with Hunt's Ketchup and has appeared in Call of Duty videos and local car commercials.[xxxvii]

Chapter 6: Legacy and Future

Patrick Mahomes has inspired young athletes everywhere for not just his play on the field, but his actions off the field. From helping kids out at the hospital, to his 15 and the Mahomies Foundation, to mentoring new players that come on the team, Mahomes is a growing legend in the game of football and in life.

The best part is, the journey has just begun and Mahomes is hungrier than ever to get better. He wants to be the best, and he has got his eye on more Super Bowl rings. How many rings? Well, he's got an idea.

"I don't know if there's a number," Mahomes said. "I mean obviously you try to chase greatness, and [Brady's] got six, so I'm going to try to do whatever I can to at least get to that number."[xxxviii]

That is one thing about the best: they always want to achieve more. They are super competitive, and they challenge themselves to go a step above and beyond what they already have. There is no end to their aspirations. Mahomes admits that he knows it is going to be difficult to get to Brady's mark, which could grow even more if he finds success in Tampa Bay, but he loves the challenge. He loves the opportunity to get better. He loves the opportunity to grow his legacy and become one of the greatest ever.

So far in his 31 career starts, Mahomes has thrown for 9,412 yards and 76 touchdowns. His passer rating of 108.9 tops all starting quarterbacks since 2017. In comparison, Tom Brady threw for just 6,613 yards and 46 touchdowns in his first 31 starts as a pro while accumulating a passer rating in the 80s. Hall of Famer Joe Montana threw for 7,700 yards in his first 31 starts and threw 51 touchdowns. Peyton Manning threw for 7,600 yards and had 52 touchdowns in his first 31 starts.[xxxix]

The quarterback that rivals Mahomes most for his starts is Dan Marino. In Marino's first full season starting in the NFL, he threw for 5,084 yards and 48 touchdowns. While that is just under what Mahomes had in his first full season as a starter, Marino had just under 9,000 yards passing in his first 31 games as a starter, close to what Mahomes had. Marino had five seasons in his first nine as a starter where he threw for at least 4,000 yards.[xl]

Mahomes is also only the eighth quarterback in history to throw for more than 5,000 yards in a season when he accomplished that mark in 2018, and he was the first to do it in his first 16 starts (if you add the last game of 2017 and take away the final game of 2018). The other quarterbacks to achieve that mark were Dan Marino, Drew Brees (who did it twice), Tom Brady, Peyton Manning, Matthew Stafford, and Ben Roethlisberger. Mahomes is only the second player to do it while also throwing for 50 touchdowns in that season; Peyton Manning is the only other to accomplish that incredible feat.[xl]

And what separates Mahomes from most other legendary quarterbacks is his ability to run. Brady, Marino, Manning, and Montana were not mobile quarterbacks. Brees and Roethlisberger were not afraid to use their legs but still didn't have the impressive mobility that Mahomes does. Mahomes has run for 500 yards in his 31 career starts. His 272 rushing yards to go along with his 5,097 yards passing in 2018 puts him fourth-most ever on the list for all-purpose passing and rushing yards in a season.[xl]

Mahomes does not necessarily have the mobility that guys like Randall Cunningham, Steve McNair, Michael Vick, and Cam Newton, but they never came anywhere close to the passing numbers that Mahomes is achieving. The closest comparison for dual-threat quarterbacks may be Warren Moon, who threw for almost 4,700 yards while rushing for 215.[xl]

When it comes to winning, Mahomes is most compared with Brady and Montana. Thus far, he is 24-

7 in his career as a starter and has a Super Bowl ring. Brady was 34-12 with two Super Bowl rings in his first three full seasons as a starter, including a Super Bowl ring in his first year as a starter. Montana's first full season as a starter, he went 13-3 and won a Super Bowl. Two seasons later, he went 10-6, then 14-1, and added another ring. Mahomes will no doubt be seeking to join Brady and Montana as the youngest quarterbacks to have two Super Bowl rings.[xxxix]

When you are talking about everything combined, including arm strength, winning, mobility, character, and clutch performances, it is hard to argue against Mahomes being the greatest quarterback ever in two full seasons as a starter. Brady may have won more, but his arm strength and mobility was nowhere near Mahomes.' What he is doing is incredible, and he is on pace to crush countless records if he can hang on to this pace for years to come.

Mahomes has a lot of great advice for young athletes everywhere. He recently said, "Every experience, good or bad, you have to learn from. I just try to learn from every mistake that I make so that I never make them again."[xxxiii] In other words, you should constantly be learning. Just because you make a mistake, do not be discouraged or let it get you down. Instead, break down what you did wrong, learn from your mistake, and get better because of it. It is about attitude. Mahomes is successful because of his mental game just as much as his physical. Hardly do you see him display any sort of temper on the field, even at the most difficult moments. He is passionate and shows that passion on the field, but when he makes mistakes, you never see him throwing his helmet or yelling at others. Instead, he acknowledges it with grace and he learns from it.

Mahomes also tells young athletes to be the best you can be and do not change who you are. Be yourself. Patrick Mahomes has always said, "I try to be the best

Patrick Mahomes I can be."[xxxiii] Every youngster needs to have that same mentality. Have your role models, but play your own game, not someone else's.

At just 24 years of age, it is almost certain that Mahomes has many more MVPs in him, many more AFC Championships, many more Pro Bowls, and perhaps more Super Bowls. And he certainly has many more records in his sights. Touchdown records, yardage records, and completion records are likely to be challenged by Mahomes, who hopes to play for another 20 years, well into his 40s, much like Drew Brees and Tom Brady are doing. If he is able to play that long, he undoubtedly will have a memorable list of accomplishments in the record books.

Mahomes' superstar career is just getting underway.

Conclusion

You are never too young to start. Just because you may not have thrown a football yet does not mean you cannot become a football star. Or if you have not picked up a golf club yet, it does not mean you cannot make the PGA Tour one day. Patrick Mahomes has shown that you can do anything you want to if you believe in it. A quarterback that was doubted by so many scouts and experts because he never played quarterback until his sophomore year in high school, Mahomes has excelled above anyone's wildest expectations, except his.

The genes have helped. Having his father, a professional baseball player, guide him and show him the ropes helped make him who he is. His parents brought him up the right way, but most importantly, he brought *himself* up the right way. It takes two. Obviously having the right parents is crucial, but also, the child needs to have the determination and

111

willingness to do the right thing in life and be motivated to excel.

Whether Mahomes becomes the greatest quarterback of this generation or not, only time will tell. However, he has already become one of the greatest role models of any athlete out there. Patrick Mahomes II is someone every young athlete should pay attention to. His positive attitude, his humility, his willingness to get better, his character, and his helpful nature is why he is the most talked-about athlete in the world today.

And the story is just beginning…

Final Word/About the Author

I was born and raised in Norwalk, Connecticut. Growing up, I could often be found spending many nights watching basketball, soccer, and football matches with my father in the family living room. I love sports and everything that sports can embody. I believe that sports are one of the most genuine forms of competition, heart, and determination. I write my works to learn more about influential athletes in the hopes that from my writing, you the reader can walk away inspired to put in an equal if not greater amount of hard work and perseverance to pursue your goals. If you enjoyed *Patrick Mahomes: The Inspiring Story of One of Football's Superstar Quarterbacks*, please leave a review! Also, you can read more of my works on *David Ortiz, Mike Trout, Bryce Harper, Jackie Robinson, Aaron Judge, Odell Beckham Jr., Bill Belichick, Serena Williams, Rafael Nadal, Roger Federer, Novak Djokovic, Richard Sherman, Andrew Luck, Rob Gronkowski, Brett Favre, Calvin Johnson,*

Drew Brees, J.J. Watt, Colin Kaepernick, Aaron Rodgers, Peyton Manning, Tom Brady, Russell Wilson, Odell Beckham Jr., Bill Belichick, Charles Barkley, Trae Young, Gregg Popovich, Pat Riley, John Wooden, Steve Kerr, Brad Stevens, Red Auerbach, Doc Rivers, Erik Spoelstra, Michael Jordan, LeBron James, Kyrie Irving, Klay Thompson, Stephen Curry, Kevin Durant, Russell Westbrook, Anthony Davis, Chris Paul, Blake Griffin, Kobe Bryant, Joakim Noah, Scottie Pippen, Carmelo Anthony, Kevin Love, Grant Hill, Tracy McGrady, Vince Carter, Patrick Ewing, Karl Malone, Tony Parker, Allen Iverson, Hakeem Olajuwon, Reggie Miller, Michael Carter-Williams, John Wall, James Harden, Tim Duncan, Steve Nash, Draymond Green, Kawhi Leonard, Dwyane Wade, Ray Allen, Pau Gasol, Dirk Nowitzki, Jimmy Butler, Paul Pierce, Manu Ginobili, Pete Maravich, Larry Bird, Kyle Lowry, Jason Kidd, David Robinson, LaMarcus Aldridge, Derrick Rose, Paul George, Kevin Garnett, Chris Paul, Marc Gasol, Yao Ming, Al Horford,

Amar'e Stoudemire, DeMar DeRozan, Isaiah Thomas, Kemba Walker, Chris Bosh, Andre Drummond, JJ Redick, DeMarcus Cousins, Wilt Chamberlain, Bradley Beal, Rudy Gobert, Aaron Gordon, Kristaps Porzingis, Nikola Vucevic, Andre Iguodala, Devin Booker, John Stockton, Jeremy Lin, Chris Paul, Pascal Siakam, Jayson Tatum, Gordon Hayward, Nikola Jokic, Bill Russell, Victor Oladipo, Luka Doncic, Ben Simmons, Shaquille O'Neal, Joel Embiid, Donovan Mitchell, Damian Lillard and *Giannis Antetokounmpo* in the Kindle Store. If you love football, check out my website at claytongeoffreys.com to join my exclusive list where I let you know about my latest books and give you lots of goodies.

Like what you read? Please leave a review!

I write because I love sharing the stories of influential athletes like Patrick Mahomes with fantastic readers like you. My readers inspire me to write more so please do not hesitate to let me know what you thought by leaving a review! If you love books on life, sports, or productivity, check out my website at claytongeoffreys.com to join my exclusive list where I let you know about my latest books. Aside from being the first to hear about my latest releases, you can also download a free copy of *33 Life Lessons: Success Principles, Career Advice & Habits of Successful People*. See you there!

Clayton

References

[i] "2017 NFL Draft." *Pro-Football Reference.* Nd. Web.

[ii] Roesch, Wesley. "Brett Veach: Mahomes is One of the Best Players I've Ever Seen." *Chiefs Wire.* 1 Mar 2018. Web.

[iii] "Pat Mahomes Stats." Baseball-Reference. Nd. Web.

[iv] "Patrick Mahomes Biography Facts, Childhood, and Personal Life." *Sporty Tell.* 3 Feb 2020. Web.

[iv] Sweeney, Eric. "Andy Reid's Quote About Patrick Mahomes Tells You Everything You Need to Know About Super Bowl LIV." *SB Nation.* 1 Feb 2020. Web.

[v] "Patrick Mahomes Childhood Story Plus Untold Biography Facts." *Childhood Biography.* 30 Jun 2020. Web.

[vi] Fishman, Jon. "Sports All-Stars: Patrick Mahomes." *Lerner Publications.* 2020. Print.

[vii] "Patrick Mahomes Reveals the Athletes He Idolized as a Child." *Heavy.com.* Nd. Web.

[viii] Gamble, J.R. "Patrick Mahomes Jr.'s Dad Chronicles His Son's NFL Rise to $500 Million Man." *The Shadow League.* 13 Jul 2020. Web.

[ix] Joyce, Grey. "Chiefs Patrick Mahomes was Wowing Pros at 5 Years Old." *The New York Post.* 23 Jan 2020. Web.

[x] Nightengale, Bob. "Patrick Mahomes—the NFL's Hottest QB—Grew Up in Major League Clubhouses." *USA Today.* 18 Sep 2018.

[xi] Kilgore, Adam. "Patrick Mahomes Became the NFL's Best Quarterback by Refusing to Specialize at Quarterback." *The Washington Post.* 30 Jan 2020. Web.

[xii] Pielucci, Mike. "Why Was Patrick Mahomes Not in High Demand Coming Out of High School." *Bleacher Report.* 12 Dec 2018. Web.

[xiii] "Patrick Mahomes' High School Football Stats." *MaxPreps.* Nd. Web.

[xiv] Andrew, Scottie. "Patrick Mahomes' Classmate Predicted He'd Win the Super Bowl Ring in their High School Yearbook. Six Years Later, It Came True. *CNN*.com. 5 Feb 2020. Web.

[xv] Beck, Jason. "How Patrick Mahomes Could've Ended up a Tiger." *MLB*.com. 20 Jan 2020. Web.

xvi Clair, Michael. "What If? Inside Patrick Mahomes' Baseball Stint." *MLB.com.* 30 Jan 2020. Web.

xvii Jacobson, Kyle. "Patrick Mahomes' Top Five Games at Texas Tech." *SB Nation.* 11 Jan 2017. Web.

xviii Al-Khateeb, Zac. "Patrick Mahomes College Timeline, From Multi-Sport HS Stardom to Texas Tech Highlight Machine." *Sporting News.* Nd. Web.

xix "Patrick Mahomes College Stats." *Sports-Reference.* Nd. Web.

xx Davis, Scott. "Patrick Mahomes Flashed his Greatness Before the NFL Draft with an 80-yard Throw During a Workout That Made Scouts Gush." *Business Insider.* 3 Feb 2020. Web.

xxi Teicher, Adam. "Drafting Patrick Mahomes: How the Chiefs Outmaneuvered the NFL." *ESPN.* 21 Apr 2019. Web.

xxii Shrock, John. "How Alex Smith Helped Chiefs' Patrick Mahomes Develop in Rookie Season." *NBC Sports.* 28 Jan 2020. Web.

xxiii Maske, Mark. "Before Patrick Mahomes was a Superstar, he Followed a Blueprint Set by Alex Smith." *The Washington Post.* 29 Jan 2020. Web.

xxiv Teicher, Adam. "Legend of Patrick Mahomes Began with Ridiculous Throws in Denver." *ESPN.* 17 Oct 2019.

xxv Rapp, Timothy. "Chiefs' Patrick Mahomes Wins MVP After 50-50 Season." *The Bleacher Report.* 2 Feb 2019. Web.

xxvi "Patrick Mahomes: Breaking Down the NFL MVP's Mind-Blowing 2018 Season." *Athlon Sports.* 23 Jul 2019. Web.

xxvii Larrabee, Kirk. "Top 15 Patrick Mahomes Moments of the 2018 Season." *247 Sports.* 3 Jan 2019. Web.

xxviii Kirkhoff, Blair. "Wow: Check Out All the Records Broken by Patrick Mahomes and the Chiefs Offense." *The Kansas City Star.* 9 Jan 2019. Web.

xxix Goldman, Charles. "Chiefs QB Patrick Mahomes Continues to Break NFL Records." *Chiefs Wire.* 11 Nov 2019. Web.

xxx Kilgore, Adam and Bieler, Des. "Patrick Mahomes Erases Huge Deficit vs. Texas, Leads Chiefs Back to AFC Title Game." *The Washington Post.* 12 Jan 2020.

xxxi "Mahomes' Feet, Arms Lift Chiefs to Super Bowl Over Titans." *The Associated Press.* 19 Jan 2020. Web.

xxxii D'Andrea, Christian. "Patrick Mahomes Turned Around a Distrastrous Game to Win Super Bowl MVP." *SB Nation.* 2 Feb 2020. Web.

xxxiii McLeod, Nia Simone. "50 Patrick Mahomes Quotes from the Super Bowl MVP." EveryDayPower.com. 16 Apr 2020. Web.

xxxiv McLaughlin, Kelly. "Patrick Mahomes and his Girlfriend Brittany Matthews are High School Sweethearts Who Have Both Built Their Sports Empires." *Business Insider.* 29 Jan 2020. Web.

xxxv Williams, Paul. "10 Things You Didn't Know About Patrick Mahomes." Clutch Sports. 26 Sep 2018.

xxxvi "15 and the Mahomes Foundation." 15andtheMahomes.org. Nd. Web.

xxxvii Chang, Ellen. "What is Patrick Mahomes' Net Worth?" TheStreet.com. Nd. Web.

xxxviii Kasabian, Paul. "Chiefs Patrick Mahomes Says He's Chasing Tom Brady's Legacy, 6 Super Bowl Rings." *The Bleacher Report.* 10 Jul 2020. Web.

xxxix Patrick Mahomes NFL Stats." Pro-Football Reference. Nd. Web.

xl Camarillo, Pete. "Is There Any Quarterback in History Similar to Patrick Mahomes?" *ClutchPoints.com.* 2019. Web.

Made in the USA
Las Vegas, NV
07 February 2023

67084479R00069